danger on peaks

Books by Gary Snyder

Gary Snyder

# danger on peaks

poems

Shoemaker S&H Hoard *Washington, D.C.*

Library of Congress Cataloging-in-Publication Data
Snyder, Gary, 1930–
Danger on Peaks : poems / Gary Snyder.
p. cm.
Includes bibliographical references.
ISBN 1-59376-041-8
I. Title.
PS3569.N88D36 2004
811'.54—dc22      2004011649

Text design by David Bullen
Printed in the United States of America

Shoemaker 〖S⁄H〗 Hoard
A Division of Avalon Publishing Group Inc.
Distributed by Publishers Group West

10  9  8  7  6  5  4  3  2

For Carole

*". . . danger on peaks"*

# Contents

## V.   Dust in the Wind

## VI.  After Bamiyan

# danger on peaks

# I

## Mount St. Helens

*Loowit*

from Sahaptin / lawilayt-Lá / "Smoker, Smoky"

# ▫ The Mountain

From the doab of the Willamette and the Columbia, slightly higher ground, three snowpeaks can be seen when it's clear—Mt. Hood, Mt. Adams, and Mt. St. Helens. A fourth, Mt. Rainier, farther away, is only visible from certain spots. In a gentle landscape like the western slope, snowpeaks hold much power, with their late afternoon or early morning glow, light play all day, and always snow. The Columbia is a massive river with a steady flow. Those peaks and the great river, and the many little rivers, set the basic form of this green wooded Northwest landscape. Whether suburban, rural, or urban the rivers go through it and the mountains rise above.

Mt. St. Helens, "Loowit" (said to be the "Indian name")—a perfect snowcapped volcanic cone, rising from almost sea level to (back then) 9,677 feet. I always wanted to go there. Hidden on the north side in a perched basin is a large deep lake.

## Spirit Lake

When I first saw Spirit Lake I was thirteen. It was clear and still, faint wisps of fog on the smooth silvery surface, encircled by steep hills of old fir. The paved road ended at the outlet, right by the Spirit Lake Lodge. A ways down the dirt road was a little shingle Forest Service Ranger Station. Farther down was a camp.

Looking out on the lake and across, only forested hills. Cool silence. South of the ranger station a dirt road climbed steadily up to a lighter drier zone. It was three miles to timberline. The mountain above the lake: they reflected each other. Maybe the mountain in the lake survives.

The camp had tent platforms under the big trees in a web of soft fir-floor trails. They were all near the water. It was so dark on the forest floor that there was almost no undergrowth, just a few skinny huckleberries. The camp had a big solid wood and stone kitchen building, and a simple half-open dining hall. There was one two-story lodge in the rustic stone and log construction that flourished (making work for skilled carpenters) during the Depression.

From the camp by the lake we went out on several-day hikes. Loading Trapper Nelson packboards, rolling our kapok sleeping bags tight, and dividing the loads of groceries and blackened #10 can cook pots with wire bail handles. The trails took us around the lake and up to the ridges: Coldwater Mt. Lookout and on to Mt. Margaret and beyond, into a basin of lakes and snowfields nestled below. From the ridges we could look back to Spirit Lake and the mountain with its symmetry and snowfields. We walked through alpine flowers, kicked steps traversing snowfields, glissaded down and settled in by rocky lakes to boisterous campsites and smoky crusty tincan meals all cooked by boys.

# The Climb

Walking the nearby ridges and perching on the cliffs of Coldwater Mountain, I memorized the upper volcano. The big and little Lizards (lava ridges with their heads uphill), the Dogshead, with a broad bulge of brown rock and white snowpatches making it look faintly like a St. Bernard. The higher-up icefields with the schrund and wide crevasses, and the approach slopes from timberline. Who wouldn't take the chance to climb a snowpeak and get the long view?

Two years later the chance came. Our guide was a old-time Mazama from Tigard in Oregon. His climbing life went back to World War One. Then he got a big orchard. He wore a tall black felt hunting hat, high corked loggers-boots, stagged-off pants, and carried the old style alpenstock. We put white zinc oxide paste on our noses and foreheads, each got our own alpenstock, and we wore metal-rimmed dark goggles like Sherpas in the thirties. We set out climbing the slidey pumice lower slopes well before dawn.

Step by step, breath by breath—no rush, no pain. Onto the snow on Forsyth Glacier, over the rocks of the Dogshead, getting a lesson in alpenstock self-arrest, a talk on safety and patience, and then on to the next phase: ice. Threading around crevasses, climbing slow, we made our way to the summit just like Issa's

> "Inch by inch
> little snail
> creep up Mt. Fuji"

West Coast snowpeaks are too much! They are too far above the surrounding lands. There is a break between. They are in a different world. If you want to get a view of the world you live in, climb a little rocky mountain with a neat small peak. But the big snowpeaks pierce the realm of clouds and cranes, rest in the zone of five-colored banners and writhing crackling dragons in veils of ragged mist and frost-crystals, into a pure transparency of blue.

St. Helens' summit is smooth and broad, a place to nod, to sit and write, to watch what's higher in the sky and do a little dance. Whatever the numbers say, snowpeaks are always far higher than the highest airplanes ever get. I made my petition to the shapely mountain, "Please help this life." When I tried to look over and down to the world below—*there was nothing there.*

And then we grouped up to descend. The afternoon snow was perfect for glissade and leaning on our stocks we slid and skidded between cracks and thumps into soft snow, dodged lava slabs, got into the open snowfield slopes and almost flew to the soft pumice ridges below. Coming down is so fast! Still high we walked the three-mile dirt road back to the lake.

# Atomic Dawn

The day I first climbed Mt. St. Helens was August 13, 1945.

Spirit Lake was far from the cities of the valley and news came slow. Though the first atomic bomb was dropped on Hiroshima August 6 and the second dropped on Nagasaki August 9, photographs didn't appear in the *Portland Oregonian* until August 12. Those papers must have been driven in to Spirit Lake on the 13th. Early the morning of the 14th I walked over to the lodge to check the bulletin board. There were whole pages of the paper pinned up: photos of a blasted city from the air, the estimate of 150,000 dead in Hiroshima alone, the American scientist quoted saying "nothing will grow there again for seventy years." The morning sun on my shoulders, the fir forest smell and the big tree shadows; feet in thin moccasins feeling the ground, and my heart still one with the snowpeak mountain at my back. Horrified, blaming scientists and politicians and the governments of the world, I swore a vow to myself, something like, "By the purity and beauty and permanence of Mt. St. Helens, I will fight against this cruel destructive power and those who would seek to use it, for all my life."

## ▫ Some Fate

Climbed Loowit — Sahaptin name — three more times.
July of '46 with sister Thea
(went to Venezuela & Cartagena as a seaman summer of 1948)
June of '49 with dear friend Robin who danced shimmering in the
snow, and again with her late that summer

This wide Pacific land     blue haze edges
mists and far gleams     broad Columbia River
eastern Pacific somewhere west
us at a still place     in the wheel of the day
right at home at     the gateway to nothing
can only keep going.

Sit on a rock and gaze out into space
leave names in the summit book,
prepare to descend

on down to some fate in the world

## 1980: Letting Go

Centuries, years and months of—

let off a little steam
cloud up and sizzle
growl      stamp-dance
quiver     swell, glow
glare      bulge

swarms of earthquakes, tremors, rumbles

*she goes*
   8.32 AM  18 May 1980

superheated steams and gasses
white-hot crumbling boulders lift and fly in a
burning sky-river wind of
searing lava droplet hail,
huge icebergs in the storm, exploding mud,
shoots out flat and rolls a swelling billowing
cloud of rock bits,
crystals, pumice, shards of glass
dead ahead blasting away—
a heavenly host of tall trees goes flat down
lightning dances through the giant smoke

a calm voice on the two-way
ex-navy radioman and volunteer
describes the spectacle—then
says, the hot black cloud is
rolling toward him—no way
but wait his fate

*II*

a photographer's burnt camera
full of half melted pictures,
three fallers and their trucks
chainsaws in back, tumbled gray and still,
two horses swept off struggling in hot mud
a motionless child laid back in a stranded ashy pickup

roiling earth-gut-trash cloud tephra twelve miles high
ash falls like snow on wheatfields and orchards to the east
five hundred Hiroshima bombs

in Yakima, darkness at noon

# □ Blast Zone

Late August 2000.
An early plane from Reno to Portland, meet Fred Swanson at the baggage claim. Out of the Portland airport and onto these new streets, new highways, there's a freeway bridge goes right across the Columbia, the 205, piers touch down on the mid-river island, but there's no way onto it. This is the skinny cottonwood island that Dick Meigs and I used to sail to and camp on the sandbars. Blackberries growing around the transmission towers.

In an instant we're in Washington State, and swinging north to join the main 5. Signs for Battleground, Cougar. Crossing the Lewis River, the Columbia to the left, the Kalama River, the old Trojan nuke plant towers, then on to Castle Rock. Freeway again, no sign of the towns — they're off to the west — and we turn into the Toutle River valley on a big new road. Old road, old bridges most all swept away.

(Remembering two lane highway 99, and how we'd stop for groceries in Castle Rock, a hunter/logger's bar with walls covered solid by racks of antlers. The road east toward Spirit Lake first climbed steeply out of town and then gradually up along the river. It was woodlots and pasture and little houses and barns, subsistence farms, farmer-loggers.) Air cool, clear day, bright green trees.

The new Silver Lake Mt. St. Helens Visitors Center is close enough to the freeway that travelers on the 5 can swing by here, take a look, and continue on. It's spacious, with a small movie theater in back and a volcano model in the center large enough to descend into, walk through, and at the center look down a skillful virtual rising column of molten magma coming up from the core of the earth.

The Center's crowded with people speaking various languages. Gazing around at the photographs and maps, I begin to get a sense of what transformations have been wrought. The Toutle River *lahar* made it all the way to the Columbia River, some sixty miles, and deposited enough ash and mud into the main channel to block shipping until it was dredged, weeks later.

We go on up the highway. Swanson explains how all the agencies wanted to get in on the restoration money that was being raised locally (and finally by Congress). They each put forth proposals: the Soil Conservation Service wanted to drop $16.5 million worth of grass seed and fertilizer over the whole thing, the Forest Service wanted to salvage-log and replant trees, and the Army Corps of Engineers wanted to build sediment retention dams. (They got to do some.) The Forest Ecology Mind (incarnated in many local people, the environmental public, and some active scientists) prevailed, and within the declared zone, zero restoration became the rule. Let natural succession go to work and take its time. Fred Swanson was trained as a geologist, then via soils went into forest and stream ecology research in the Andrews Forest in Oregon. He has been studying Mt. St. Helens from the beginning.

The Corps of Engineers went to work along the Toutle with hundreds of giant trucks and earth movers. Swanson takes a turn off the main road, just a few miles on, to a view of an earthwork dam that was built to help hold back further debris floods in the new river channel. The lookout parking lot had clearly been more of a tourist destination in the past than it is now, partly closed and getting overgrown with alders. Once the dump trucks stopped, the people didn't come so much to look. But there it is, lots of earth holding back what further mud and gravel might be coming down—for a while.

The color of the dam, the riverbanks, the roads, is "volcano-ash-gray." New bridges, new road, this has all been rebuilt. Swanson says that for some years after the eruption there was no access into the west side of Spirit Lake. To get closer to the lake and the mountain, people were driving a string of small roads north and around. You could drive up from the east to Windy Ridge. And then a new state highway from the 5 to the west side ridge above the lake got built. You still can't drive to the edge of the lake—all pumice, ash, and broken rock.

The new road is an expensive accomplishment. It runs above the old Toutle riverbed along the hillside with fancy bridges, then into the Coldwater Creek drainage (I hiked down this when it was old-growth forest, and trail was the only access); makes a big curve around the head of the valley and does a long switchback climb. In that upper cirque of Coldwater Creek there are plenty of old gray logs lying tossed about on the ground. Between and around the logs the hills are aflower in fireweed and pearly everlasting *Anaphalis margaritacea*. Little silver fir three to ten feet high are tucked in behind the logs, mixed in with the tall flowers.

Finally pull up to the high ridge, now named Johnston after the young geologist who died there, and walk to the edge. The end of the road. Suddenly there's all of Loowit and a bit of the lake basin! In a new shape, with smoking scattered vents in this violet-gray light.

> The white dome peak whacked lower down,
> open-sided crater on the northside, fumarole wisps
> a long gray fan of all that slid and fell
> angles down clear to the beach
> dark old-growth forest gone    no shadows
> the lake afloat with white bone blowdown logs
> scoured ridges round the rim, bare outcrop rocks
> squint in the bright
> ridgetop plaza packed with puzzled visitor gaze
>
> no more White Goddess
> but,    under the fiery sign of Pele,
> and Fudo—Lord of Heat
> who sits on glowing lava with his noose
> lassoing hardcore types
> from hell against their will,
>
> Luwit, lawilayt-lá—*Smoky*
> is her name

## □ To Ghost Lake

Walk back down from the west side view ridge and drive back to
Castle Rock and the 5. Start a drive-circumambulation of the moun-
tain, going north and then east up the Cowlitz Valley. The Cowlitz
River gets some of its water from the south side glaciers of Mt.
Rainier and the northwest side of Mt. Adams. Dinner at "Carter's
Roadhouse"—old place, slow and funky service, a bar, small press
local history books for sale. Then swing south on a forest road to the
Iron Creek Campground on the Cispus River and lay out ground-
sheet in the dark.

Next morning walk the gravelly bar of the little Cispus, duck under
droops of moss from old-growth cedar, hot tea on the fir needles.
Drive to the Boundary Trail, winding higher on ridgerunning tracks,
break out around a corner and there's the mountain and then
suddenly we are in the Blast Zone.

In a great swath around the lake basin, everything in direct line to
the mountain is flat down: white clear logs, nothing left standing.
Next zone of tree-suffering is dead snags still upright. Then a zone
called "ashed trees" blighted by a fall of ash, but somehow alive.
Last, lucky to be out of line with the blast, areas of green forest
stand. A function of distance, direction, and slope. Finally, far
enough back, healthy old forest stretches away.

New patterns march in from the edges, while within the zone
occasional little islands of undamaged vegetation survive. In some
cases a place still covered with snow and down in a dip. From Windy
Ridge the carpet of floating logs on the lake is mostly at the north
end.

Go out several miles walking along the ridge and onto slopes of the
volcano. It's all ash and rock now, no forest regrowth here, and the
sun as hot and dry as Arizona.

At the car again and drive to the Norway Pass road turnoff (from the mountain road see an arrow, shot and sticking in a dead tree, up high, and from the downslope side. Why? How?) and go north for a look down at the Green River valley and beyond that the high Goat Mountain ridge. Too far north up there to be affected. Down in the Green River valley one can see the distinct boundary between the unmanaged "ecological zone" of the Volcanic Monument where natural succession rules, and the adjacent National Forest land that had soon been logged and planted. The planting took hold well. In the natural succession blast zone the conifers are rising — not quite tall enough to shade out down logs and flowers, but clearly flourishing. But over into the "planted" zone it's striking to see how much taller and denser the growing plantation is. Well, no surprise. Wild natural process takes time, and allows for the odd and unexpected. We still know far too little about it. This natural regeneration project has special values of its own, aesthetic, spiritual, scientific. Both the wild and the managed sides will be instructive to watch for centuries to come.

Baby plantlife, spiky, firm and tender,
stiffly shaking in the same old breeze.

We camped for the night on a ridgetop with long views both ways. A tiny fire, a warm breeze, cloudless starry sky. The faint whiffs of sulfur from the fumaroles. In the morning, cloud-fog rising covers the sun. Fog comes up the Columbia Valley and fills the deep-cut side-canyons clear back to here — floats awhile past our nearby truck.

Sit on folded groundsheets on the ashy pumice hard-packed soil and pick up our conversations again. Fred clarifies distinctions such as "original" and "restored." What's old? What's new? What's "renew"? I then held forth on the superiority of the Han'-gul writing system of Korea over all other alphabets, but what got me started on that? Our hissing Primus stove. I talked about ten years of living in Japan, "Two hundred miles of industrial city-strip along the railroad, and tenth-growth forest mountains far as you can see. Went twice through Hiroshima, great noodles, full of activists, green and leafy —doing fine."

Fred's mind is as open as a summer morning in the Sierra. We talk about a lot. But when we come back to forests, eruptions, and the balance of economy and ecology, I shut up and listen.

Green tea hotwater
Sunball in the fog
Loowit cooled in white
New crater summit lightly dusted
Morning fumarole summit mist-wisps—"Hah" . . . "Hah"

One final trip before leaving: a walk to Ghost Lake: pearly everlasting, huckleberries and fireweed, all the way.

Out to Ghost Lake through white snags,
threading down tree deadfalls, no trail work lately here,
light chaco sandals leaping, nibbling huckleberries, walking logs
bare toed dusty feet
I worked around this lake in '49
both green then

## □ Pearly Everlasting

Walk a trail down to the lake
mountain ash and elderberries red
old-growth log bodies blown about,
whacked down, tumbled in the new ash *wadis*.
Root-mats tipped up, veiled in tall straight fireweed,
fields of prone logs laid by blast
in-line north-south down and silvery
limbless barkless poles —
clear to the alpine ridgetop all you see
is toothpicks of dead trees
thousands of summers
at detritus-cycle rest
— hard and dry in the sun — the long life of the down tree yet to go
bedded in bushes of pearly everlasting
dense white flowers
saplings of bushy vibrant silver fir
the creek here once was "Harmony Falls"
The pristine mountain
just a little battered now
the smooth dome gone
ragged crown

the lake was shady *yin* —
now blinding water mirror of the sky
remembering days of fir and hemlock —
no blame to magma or the mountain
& sit on a clean down log at the the lake's edge,
the water dark as tea.

I had asked Mt. St. Helens for help
the day I climbed it,     so seems she did

The trees all lying flat like,      after that big party
Siddhartha went to on the night he left the house for good,
crowd of young friends whipped from sexy dancing
dozens crashed out on the floor

angelic boys and girls, sleeping it off.
A palace orgy of the gods but what
"we" see is "Blast Zone" sprinkled with
clustered white flowers

"Do not be tricked by human-centered views," says Dogen,
And Siddhartha looks it over, slips away—for another forest—
—to really get right down on life and death.

*If you ask for help it comes.*
But not in any way you'd ever know
—thank you Loowit, lawilayt-lá, *Smoky Mâ*
                    gracias      xiexie      grace

## ◻ Enjoy the Day

One morning on a ridgetop east of Loowit
after campstove coffee

looking at the youthful old volcano
breathing steam and sulfur
sunrise lava
bowls of snow

went up behind a mountain hemlock
asked my old advisors where they lay

what's going on?

they say

"New friends and dear sweet old tree ghosts
       here we are again. Enjoy the day."

# II

## Yet Older Matters

## Hanging Out by Putah Creek with Younger Poets

*Sitting on the dusty*
*dry-leaf crackly ground,*
*freeway rumble south,*
*black walnut shade,*
*crosslegged, hot,*
        *exchanging little poems*

## Yet Older Matters

A rain of black rocks        out of space
onto deep blue ice      in Antarctica
nine thousand feet high        scattered for miles.

Crunched inside      yet older matter
from times before our very sun

*(from a conversation with Eldridge Moores*
*& Kim Stanley Robinson)*

## Flowers in the Night Sky

I thought, forest fires burning to the north!
yellow nomex jacket thrown in the cab, hard-hat, boots,
I gunned the truck up the dirt-road scrambling,
and came out on a flat stretch with a view:
shimmering blue-green streamers and a red glow down the sky—
Stop. Storms on the sun. Solar winds going by

*(The night of the red aurora borealis:*
*seen as far south as northern California, April 2001)*


## A Dent in a Bucket

Hammering a dent out of a bucket
    a woodpecker
        answers from the woods

## Baby Jackrabbit

Baby jackrabbit on the ground
thick furry brindled coat
little black tailtip
back of the neck ate out,
life for an owl.

## Work Day

They want—
Short lengths of 1" schedule 40 PVC
A 10' chimney sweeping brush
someone to grind the mower blades
a log chain,
my neighbors' Spring work.

    Chainsaw dust
    clay-clod stuck spade
    apple blossoms and bees

## Asian Pear

The slender tender Asian pear
unpruned, skinny, by the zendo
never watered, ragged,
still puts out fruit
        fence broken,
trunk scored with curls of bark,
bent-off branches, high-up scratches —
pears for a bear


## Cool Clay

In a swarm of yellowjackets
a squirrel drinks water
feet in the cool clay, head way down

## Give Up

Walking back from the Dharma-Talk
summer dry madrone
leaves rattle down

"Give up! give up!
  Oh sure!" they say


## How

small birds      flit
from bough
to bough to bough

to bough to bough to bough

## Whack

Green pinecone flakes
pulled, gnawed clean around,
wobbling, slowly falling
scattering on the ground,
      whack the roof.
Tree-top squirrel feasts
— twitchy pine boughs.


## Yowl

Out of the underbrush
a bobcat bursts chasing a housecat.
Crash — yowl — silence.
Pine pollen settles again.

## April Calls and Colors

Green steel waste bins
flapping black plastic lids
gobbling flattened cardboard,
far off, a backup beeper

## Standup Comics

A parking meter that won't take coins
a giant sprinkler valve wheel chained and locked
a red and white fire hydrant
a young dandelion at the edge of the pavement

## Sky, Sand

Cottonwoods streambank
      splashing fording up the creekbed
black phoebe calling *pi pi pi* here, near—
Mexican blackhawk cruising—squint at the sky,
shoes full of sand

                  *(Aravaipa Canyon, Arizona)*


## Mimulus on the Road to Town

Out of cracks in the roadcut rockwalls,
clumps of peach-colored mimulus
spread and bloom,
      stiffly quiver in the hot
log-truck breeze-blast
always going by—
they never die.

## A Tercel is a Young Male Hawk

Falconers used to believe that the third hawk egg in a clutch would
be a male. So they call a young male hawk a "tercel" from *tertius*,
"third." Who knows why carmakers name their cars the way they do.

> Taking the gas cap off
> > stick it in my work vest pocket
> I see a silver Tercel parked
> by a hedge and a waste bin full of bottles
>
> — filling my old Toyota pickup.


## Brighter Yellow

An "Ozark Trucking" bigrig pulls up
by me on the freeway, such a vivid yellow!
a brighter yellow than bulldozers.
This morning James Lee Jobe was talking
        of the wild blue bonnets
and the dark red Indian paintbrush down in Texas.
Said, "from a distance — them growing all together
        makes a field of solid purple."
Hey — keep on the right side
of that yellow line

## To the Liking of Salmon

Spawning salmon dark and jerky
just below the surface ripple
shallow lower Yuba

River bed — old mining gravels
mimicking a glacier outflow
perfect for the redds below Parks Bar.

*(how hydraulic mining made the Yuba Goldfields*
*like a post-glacial river in Alaska)*

# □ Glacier Ghosts

## Late July: Five Lakes Basin & Sand Ridge, Northern Sierra

*A lake east of the east end of Sand Ridge, a sleeping site tucked under massive leaning glacial erratic propped on bedrock, bed of wood bits, bark, and cones.*

Gravelly bed below a tilted erratic,
chilly restless night,
— ants in my hair

□

Nap on a granite slab
half in shade, you can never hear enough
sound of          wind in the pines

□

Piko feared heights
went up the steep ridge on all fours.
But she went

□

Catching grasshoppers for bait
attaching them live to the hook
— I get used to it

□

a certain poet, needling
Allen Ginsberg by the campfire
"How come they all love *you*?"

□

Clumsy at first
my legs, feet, and eye     learn again to leap,
skip through the jumbled rocks

□

Starting a glissade
down a steep snowfield
they say, "Gary, don't!"
but I know my iceaxe

□

Diving in the perched lake, coming up
can see right over the outlet waterfall
distant peaks          Sierra Buttes

□

Tired, quit climbing at a small pond
made camp, slept on a slab
til the moon rose

□

ice-scrape-ponds, scraggly pines,
long views, flower mud marshes,
so many places
for a wandering boulder to settle,
forever.

□

A gift of rattlesnake
meat — packed in —
cooked on smoky coals
how did it taste?

□

Warm nights,
the lee of twisty pines —
high jets crossing the stars

□

Things spread out
rolling and unrolling, packing and unpacking,
— this painful impermanent world.

□

Exploring the Grouse Ridge — crossing through
manzanita mats from
peak to peak — scaring up grouse

□

Creek flowing out of Lake Fauchery
old white dog
caught in the fast current
— strong lads saved him

□

Coming back down the
trail from Glacier Lake
KJ lifts her T-shirt
"look, I'm getting boobs"
two tiny points, age nine.

□

Down in the meadow
west end of Sand Ridge
the mosquitos bite everyone
but Nanao and me—why?

□

## Sand Ridge

How you survived—
gravelly two mile lateral moraine of
sand and summer snow and hardy flowers
always combing the wind
that crosses range and valley from the sea.
Walk that backbone path
ghosts of the pleistocene icefields
stretching                    down and away,
both sides

# III

## Daily Life

## ▫ What to Tell, Still

Reading the galley pages of Laughlin's *Collected Poems*
with an eye to writing a comment.
How warmly J speaks of Pound,
        I think back to—

At twenty-three I sat in a lookout cabin in gray whipping wind
at the north end of the northern Cascades,
high above rocks and ice, wondering
        should I go visit Pound at St. Elizabeth's?

And studied Chinese in Berkeley, went to Japan instead.

J puts his love for women
his love for love, his devotion, his pain, his causing-of-pain,
        right out there.

I'm 63 now & I'm on my way to pick up my ten-year-old stepdaughter
        and drive the car pool.
I just finished a five-page letter to the County Supervisors
dealing with a former supervisor,
        now a paid lobbyist,
who has twisted the facts and gets paid for his lies. Do I
have to deal with this creep? I do.

James Laughlin's manuscript sitting on my desk.
Late last night reading his clear poems—
and Burt Watson's volume of translations of Su Shih,
        next in line for a comment.

September heat.
The Watershed Institute meets,
        planning more work with the B.L.M.
And we have visitors from China, Forestry guys,

who want to see how us locals are doing with our plan.
Editorials in the paper are against us,
     a botanist is looking at rare plants in the marsh.

I think of how J writes stories of his lovers in his poems —
     puts in a lot,
     it touches me,

So recklessly bold — foolish? —
to write so much about your lovers
when you're a long-time married man. Then I think,
what do I know?
     About what to say
     or not to say, what to tell, or not, to whom,
     or when,

     *still.*

(1993)

# Strong Spirit

Working on hosting Ko Un great Korean poet.
I was sitting on the floor this morning in the dark
At the Motel Eco, with my steel cup full of latte from the Roma
calendar template sketched in pencil:
student lunches, field trips in the Central Valley
waterfowl? Cold Canyon? State Library with Kevin Starr?
Charlie wants to help with speakers money so he gave us some
a cultural visitor for a week at Aggie Davis
in the flat plain valley just by Putah Creek,
which was re-routed by engineers a hundred years ago.
I'm on the phone and on the e-mail working all this out
students and poets to gather at the Cafe California
the Korean graduate student too
His field is Nineteenth Century Lit and he's probably a Christian,
but says he'll do this. Delfina, wife of Pak, a Korean Catholic,
looks distasteful at the book and says
Ko Un's a Buddhist! — I don't think she'll come to the reading.
Drive the car through a car wash — get Sierra mud off,
about to meet him at the airport, his strong wife Sang-wha
with him in flight from Seoul.
First drive to Albany and pick up Clare Yoh,
Korean Studies at Berkeley, lives near an
old style eucalyptus grove, the smell surprised me
when I visited California as a kid — I like it still.

Down to the airport meet at Customs
and now to pay respects to our friend
poet, translator, Ok-ku died last fall
her grave on the ridgetop near the sea.
Straight up a hill due west
walk a grassy knoll in the wind,
Ko Un pouring a careful trickle of *soju* on her mound,

us bowing deep bows
— spirits for the spirit, bright poet gone
then pass the cup among the living —

strong.

*(2001)*

# Sharing an Oyster With The Captain

*"On June 17, 1579, Captain Francis Drake sailed his ship, The Golden Hinde, into the*
*gulf of the Farallones of the bay that now bears his name. He sighted these white cliffs*
*and named the land Nova Albion. During his 36 day encampment in California,*
*Drake repaired his ship, established contact with local Indians, explored inland,*
*took on supplies and water, and claimed the region for Queen Elizabeth."*

Along the roadside yarrow, scotch broom, forbs,
hills of layered angled boughs like an Edo woodcut,
rare tree—bishop pine—storm-tuned,
blacktop roadbed over the native Miwok path
over the early ranches "M" and "Pierce"
　　　　—a fox dives into the brush,
wind-trimmed chaparral and
estuary salt marsh, leaning hills,
technically off the continent,
out on the sea-plate, "floating island."

—Came down from inland granite and
gold-bearing hills　　　madrone and cedar;
& from ag-fields laser land-levelers,
giant excavators—subdivision engineers
"California" hid behind the coastal wall of fog

Drake saw a glimpse of brown dry grass and gray-green pine,
came into a curve of beach. Rowed ashore,
left a scat along the tideline, cut some letters in an oak.

The "G" Ranch running Herefords,
Charley Johnson growing oysters
using a clever method from Japan,
and behind the fog wall
sunny grassy hills and swales
filled with ducks and tules.

Cruising down the narrow road-ridge
one thing we have together yet:
this Inglis — this Mericano tongue.
— Drake's Bay cliffs like Sussex —
gray and yellow siltstone, mudstone, sandstone,
undulating cliffs and valleys — days of miles of fog.

Gray-mottled bench boards lichen.
Sea gulls flat down sun-warmed
parking lot by cars.
We offer to the land and sea,
a sierra-cup of Gallo sherry,
and eat a Johnson's oyster from the jar,

offer a sip of Sack to the Captain
*and* an oyster raw:
a salute, a toast to Sir Francis Drake
from the land he never saw.

## Summer of '97

West of the square old house, on the rise that was made
when the pond was dug; where we once slept out;
where the trampoline sat,

Earth spirit please don't mind
If cement trucks grind
And plant spirits wait a while
Please come back and smile

Ditches, lines and drains
Forms and pours and hidden doors
The house begins:

Sun for power
Cedar for siding
Fresh skinned poles for framing
Gravel for crunching and
Bollingen for bucks—

Daniel peeling
Moth for singing
Matt for pounding
Bruce for pondering
Chuck for plumbering
David drywalling
        staining, crawling;
Stu for drain rock
Kurt for hot wire
Gary for cold beer
Carole for brave laugh
        til she leaves,
        crew grieves,

Gen for painting
      each window frame
      Gen-red again

Garden cucumbers for lunch
Fresh tomatoes crunch
Tor for indoor paints and grins
Ted for rooftiles
Tarpaper curls
Sawdust swirls
Trucks for hauling
Barrels for burning
Old bedrooms disappearing

Wild turkeys watching
Deer disdainful
Bullfrogs croaking,

David Parmenter for bringing
      flooring oak at night
Though his mill burned down
He's still coming round.

Cyndra tracing manzanita
On the tile wall shower,
Sliding doors
Smooth new floors —

Old house a big hall now
Big as a stable
To bang the mead-stein on the table
Robin got a room to write a poem,
& no more nights out walking to the john.

Carole finally coming home
Peeking at her many rooms.

Oak and pine trees looking on
Old Kitkitdizze house now
Has another wing—

So we'll pour a glass and sing—
This has been fun as heaven
Summer of ninety-seven.

# ◻ Really the Real

*for Ko Un and Lee Sang-wha*

Heading south down the freeway making the switch
from Business 80 east to the I-5 south,
watch those signs and lanes that split
duck behind the trucks, all going 75 at 10 am
I tell Ko Un this is the road that runs from Mexico to Canada,
right past San Diego—LA—Sacramento—Medford—Portland—
    Centralia—
Seattle—Bellingham, B.C. all the way,
the new suburban projects with cement roof tiles
neatly piled on unfinished gables,
turn onto Twin Cities Road, then Franklin Road
pull in by the sweet little almost-wild Cosumnes River
right where the Mokulumne meets it,
(*umne* a Miwok suffix meaning river)
walking out on a levee trail through cattail, tule, button-brush,
small valley oaks, algae on the streams. Hardly any birds.
Lost Slough, across the road, out on the boardwalk
—can't see much, the tules all too tall. The freeway roar,
four sandhill cranes feeding, necks down, pacing slow.
Then west on Twin Cities Road til we hit the river.
Into Locke, park, walk the crowded Second Street
all the tippy buildings' second stories leaning out,
gleaming bikes—huge BMW with exotic control panel
eat at the Locke Gardens Chinese place, Ko Un's choice,
endless tape loop some dumb music, at the next table one white couple,
a guy with a beard; at another a single black woman
with two little round headed clearly super-sharp boys.
Out and down to Walnut Grove til we find road J-11 going east
over a slough or two then south on Staten Island Road. It's straight,
the fields all flat and lots of signs that say
no trespassing, no camping, no hunting, stay off the levee.
Driving along, don't see much, I had hoped, but about to give up.

Make a turn around and stand on the shoulder, glass the field:
flat farmland—fallow—flooded with water—
full of birds. Scanning the farther sections
hundreds of sandhill cranes are pacing—then,
those gurgling sandhill crane calls are coming out of the sky
in threes, twos, fives, from all directions,
circling, counter-spinning, higher and lower,
big silver bodies, long necks, dab of red on the head,
chaotic, leaderless, harmonic, playful—what are they doing?
Splendidly nowhere thousands

And back to Davis, forty miles, forty minutes
shivering to remember        what's going on
just a few miles west of the 5:
in the wetlands, in the ongoing elder        what you might call,
*really* the real,        world.

*(October 2001, Cosumnes
and Staten Island)*

# Ankle-deep in Ashes

Ankle-deep gray muddy ash      sticky after rain
walking wet burnt forest floor
(one-armed mechanic working on a trailer-mounted generator
a little barbecue by a parked trailer,
grilling steak after ten hours checking out the diesels)
— we're clumping through slippery ashes to a sugar pine
— a planner from a private timber company
a fire expert from the State, a woman County Supervisor
a former Forest Service line officer, the regional District Ranger,
a businessman-scientist who managed early retirement and does
     good deeds,
the superintendent of the county schools,
& the supervisor of one of the most productive public forests in
     the country—
pretty high back in the mountains
after a long hot summer wildfire and a week of rain.
Drove here through miles of standing dead trees
gazed across the mountain valley,
the sweep of black snags with no needles,
stands of snags with burnt needles dangling,
patches of green trees that still look live.
They say the duff layers glowed for weeks as the fire sank down.
This noble sugar pine we came to see is green
seven feet dbh, "diameter at breast height"
first limb a hundred feet above.
The District Ranger chips four little notches
round the trunkbase, just above the ashy dust:
cambium layer dry and brown
cooked by the slow duff burn.
He says, "Likely die in three more years
but we will let it stand."
I circumambulate it and invoke, "Good luck—long life—
*Sarvamangalam*—I hope you prove him wrong"
pacing charred twigs crisscrossed on the ground.

*(Field trip to the aftermath of the Star Fire, 5 November 2001)*

# Winter Almond

Tree over and down
its root-rot clear to the air, dirt tilted
trunk limbs and twiglets crashed
on my mother's driveway — her car's barricaded
up by the house — she called last night
"I can't get out"

I left at dawn — freezing and clear,
a scatter of light snow from last week still
little Stihl arborist's chainsaw (a thrasher)
canvas knapsack of saw gear
and head for town      fishtailing ice slicks

She's in the yard in a mustard knit hat and a shawl cerise
from her prize heap of woolens
from the world's Goodwills
The tree's rotten limbs and whippy sprouts both
in a damn near dead old frame

my mother eighty-seven (still drives)
worries the danger,
the snarl of the saw chases her into the house
in the fresh clear air I move with the limbs and the trunk
crash in a sequence and piled as it goes, so,
firewood rounds *here*, and the brushpile *there*.
rake down the drive for the car — in three hours.

Inside where it's all too hot
drink chocolate and eat black bread with smoked oysters,
Lois goes over her memory of my jobs as a youth
that made me do this sort of work
when I'm really "So intellectual. But you always worked hard as a kid."

She tells me a story: herself, seventeen, part-time clerk in a store
in Seattle, the boss called her in for a scolding.
"how come you shopped there?"—a competitor's place.
—her sister worked there (my Aunt Helen)
who could get her a discount as good
 as what they had here.
The boss said "o.k. That's o.k. then," and Lois said "also
it's time for a raise." I asked did you get it?
        "I did."
So many hours at this chair
hearing tales of the years.
"I was skinny. So thin."
With her great weight now.

"Thank you son for the tree.
  You did it quick too.
  The neighbors will say
  He came right away."

Well I needed a change.
A few rounds of sound almond wood—
maybe my craft friend Holly will want them
you won't be just firewood—a bowl or a salad fork
old down
almond tree

                                        (1993)

## Mariano Vallejo's Library

Mariano Vallejo's library
was the best in the Eastern Pacific
he was reading Rousseau, Voltaire
(some bought from the ship *Leonor*)
The Yankees arrived and he welcomed them
though they drove off his horses and cattle
then one year the Casa, books and all, burned to the ground.

The old adobe east of the Petaluma River still stands.
Silvery sheds in the pastures once were chicken-coops
the new box mansions march up the slope.
At my sister's *Empty Shell* book party some retired
chicken growers walked in cuddling favorite birds.
Vallejo taught vine-growing tricks to Charles Krug
and Agostin Haraszthy—the vineyards are everywhere
but the anarchist egg growers gone.

The bed of the Bay all shallowed by mining
pre–ice age Sierra dry riverbeds
upturned for gold and the stream gravel washed off by hoses
swept to the valley in floods.
Farmers lost patience, the miners are now gone too.
New people live in the foothills.
pine-pitch and dust, poison oak.

The barnyard fence shades jimson weed,
*datura, toloache*, white trumpet flower, dark leaf.
The old ones from the world before taught care:
whoever's here, whatever language—
race, or century, be aware
that plant can scour your mind,

put all your books behind.

## □ Waiting for a Ride

Standing at the baggage passing time:
Austin Texas airport — my ride hasn't come yet.
My former wife is making websites from her home,
one son's seldom seen,
the other one and his wife have a boy and girl of their own.
My wife and stepdaughter are spending weekdays in town
so she can get to high school.
My mother ninety-six still lives alone and she's in town too,
always gets her sanity back just barely in time.
My former former wife has become a unique poet;
most of my work,
such as it is          is done.
Full moon was October second this year,
I ate a mooncake, slept out on the deck
white light beaming through the black boughs of the pine
owl hoots and rattling antlers,
Castor and Pollux rising strong
— it's good to know that the Pole Star drifts!
that even our present night sky slips away,
not that I'll see it.
Or maybe I will, much later,
some far time walking the spirit path in the sky,
that long walk of spirits — where you fall right back into the
"narrow painful passageway of the Bardo"
squeeze your little skull
and there you are again

waiting for your ride

*(October 5, 2001)*

# IV

## Steady, They Say

# Doctor Coyote When He Had a Problem

Doctor Coyote when he had a problem
took a dump. On the grass, asked his turds where they lay
what to do? They gave him good advice.

He'd say "that's just what I thought too"
And do it.       And go his way.

# □ Claws / Cause

*for Zenshin*


"Graph" is the claw-curve, carve—
        grammar a     weaving

paw track, lizard-slither, tumble of
a single boulder down. Glacier scrapes across the bedrock,
        wave-lines on the beach.

Saying, "this was me"
        scat sign of time and mood and place

language is     breath, claw, or tongue

"tongue" with all its flickers
might be a word for

hot love, and     fate.
A single kiss     a tiny cause [claws]

—such grand effects [text].

# ▫ How Many?

Australia, a group of girls at a corroboree
Lapland, reindeer herdgirls

China, the "yaktail"

Greece, the seven daughters, sisters,
or "the sailing stars"

a cluster of faint stars in Taurus,
the Pleiades,

name of a car in Japan —
"Subaru"

in Mayan — A fistful of boys —

# Loads on the Road

Stu's stubby heavy tough old yellow dump truck
parked by his place       "For Sale"
he's fine, but times and people change.

Those loads of river-run and crushed blue mine rock
in our roadbed       Stu and me
standing talking       engine idling
those days gone now,

days to come.

# Carwash Time

Looking at a gray-pine,
chunky fire-adapted cones
bunched toward the top,
a big tree there behind the tire shop

— I'm sitting on a low fence
while a wild gang does a benefit
wash-job on my daughter's car.
Tattooed and goateed white dudes,
brown and black guys,
I say "What you raising money for?"

—"The drug and alcohol halfway
house up the street"
old Ridge sedan
never been this neat

# ◻ To All the Girls Whose Ears I Pierced Back Then

*for Maggie Brown Koller*
*(among others)*


Sometimes we remember that moment:
you stood there attentive with clothespins
dangling, setting a bloodless dimple in each lobe
as I searched for a cork & the right-sized needle
& followed the quick pierce with a small gold hoop.
The only guy with an earring
back then

It didn't hurt that much
a sweetly earnest child
and a crazy country guy
with an earring and a
gray-green cast eye
and even then,
this poem.

## She Knew All About Art

She knew all about art—she was fragrant, soft,
I rode to her fine stone apartment, hid the bike in the hedge.
—We met at an opening, her lover was brilliant and rich,
first we would talk, then drift into long gentle love.
We always made love in the dark. Thirty years older than me.

## □ Coffee, Markets, Blossoms

My Japanese mother-in-law
born in America
tough with brokers
a smart trader
grew up working barefoot
in the Delta, on the farm.
Doesn't like Japan.
Sits in the early morning
by the window, coffee in hand,

gazing at cherry blossoms.
Jean Koda
needing no poem.

## In the Santa Clarita Valley

Like skinny wildweed flowers sticking up
hexagonal "Denny's" sign
starry "Carl's"
loopy "McDonald's"
eight-petaled yellow "Shell"
blue-and-white "Mobil" with a big red "O"

growing in the asphalt riparian zone
by the soft roar of the flow
                                of Interstate 5.

# ◦ Almost Okay Now

She had been in an accident: almost okay now,
but inside still recovering,
bones slow-healing — she was anxious
still fearful of cars and of men.
As I sped up the winding hill road
she shuddered — eyes beseeching me —
I slowed the car down.
Out on a high meadow under the moon,
With delicate guidance she showed me
how to make love without hurting her
and then napped awhile in my arms,

smell of sweet grass
warm night breeze

## Sus

Two pigs in a pickup sailing down the freeway
stomping with the sway,
      gaze back up the roadbed
            on their last windy ride.

Big pink ears up        looking all around,
taut broad shoulders       trim little legs,
bright and lively with their parsnip-colored skin
wind-washed earth-diggers
      snuffling in the swamps

they're not pork, they are forever *Sus:*
      breeze-braced and standing there,
                  velvet-dusty pigs.

# Day's Driving Done

Finally floating in cool water
red sun ball sinking
through a smoky dusty haze

rumble of bigrigs,
constant buzz of cars on the 5;
at the pool of Motel 6
in Buttonwillow,
south end of the giant valley,
ghost of ancient Lake Tulare

sunset      splash.

# ◻ Snow Flies, Burn Brush, Shut Down

A wide line of men in the open pine woods
diesel torches      dripping flame
lava soil     frost on the sagebrush
loggers walking from brushpile to brushpile
dark sky reddish from brushpiles burning.
At Sidwalter Butte three men on horseback
torches mounted on slender lances
crisscrossing miles of buttes and canyons

hundreds of brushpiles aflame
steady light snow.

            *(end of the season, Warm Springs, Oregon, 1954)*

# ▫ Icy Mountains Constantly Walking

*for Seamus Heaney*

Work took me to Ireland
      a twelve-hour flight.
The river Liffy;
      ale in a bar,
So many stories
      of passions and wars —
A hilltop stone tomb
      with the wind across the door.
Peat swamps go by:
      people of the ice age.
Endless fields and farms —
      the last two thousand years.

I read my poems in Galway,
      just the chirp of a bug.
And flew home thinking
      of literature and time.

The rows of books
      in the Long Hall at Trinity
The ranks of stony ranges
      above the ice of Greenland.

*(March 1995)*

## For Philip Zenshin Whalen
d. 26 June 2002

*(and for 33 pine trees)*

Load of logs on
chains cinched down and double-checked
the truck heads slowly up the hill

I bow *namaste* and farewell
these ponderosa pine
whose air and rain and sun we shared

for thirty years,
struck by beetles          needles
turning rusty brown,
and moving on.

—decking, shelving, siding,
stringers, studs, and joists,

*I will think of you          pines from this mountain*
*as you shelter people in the Valley*
*years to come*

## □ For Carole

I first saw her in the zendo
at meal time     unwrapping bowls
head forward folding back the cloth
          as server I was kneeling
to fill three sets of bowls each time
up the line
                    Her lithe leg
                    proud, skeptical,
                    passionate, trained
                    by the
                    heights     by the
                    danger on peaks

# Steady, They Say

Clambering up the rocks of a dry wash gully,
warped sandstone, by the San Juan River,

look north to stony mountains
shifting clouds and sun

—despair at how the human world goes down

Consult my old advisers

"steady" they say

"today"

*(At Slickhorn Gulch on
the San Juan River, 1999)*

# V

## Dust in the Wind

# ▫ Gray Squirrels

Three squirrels like,    dash to the end of a pine limb, leap, catch
an oak bough angling down — jump across air to another pine —
and on — forest grove canopy world "chug - chug" at each other —
scolding empty space

       Follow their path by the quivering oak leaves
       and a few pine needles floating down

# ◻ One Day in Late Summer

One day in late summer in the early nineties I had lunch with my old friend Jack Hogan, ex-longshore union worker and activist of San Francisco, at a restaurant in my small Sierra town. The owner had recently bought and torn down the adjoining brick building which had been in its time a second-hand bookstore, "3Rs," run by a puckish ex-professor. Our lunch table in the patio was right where his counter had been. Jack was married to my sister once. We all hung out in North Beach back in the fifties, but now he lives in Mexico.

> This present moment
> that lives on
>
> to become
>
> long ago

(1994)

## ▫ Spilling the Wind

The faraway line of the freeway faint murmur of motors, the slow
steady semis and darting little cars; two thin steel towers with faint
lights high up blinking; and we turn on a raised dirt road between
two flooded fallow ricefields — wind brings more roar of cars

       hundreds of white-fronted geese
       from nowhere
       spill the wind from their wings
       wobbling and sideslipping down

*(Lost Slough, Cosumnes, February 2002)*

# ◦ California Laurel

The botanist told us
"Over by Davis Lumber, between house furnishings and plumbing,
there's a Grecian laurel growing—not much smell, but that's the one
that poets wore. Now California laurel's not a laurel. It can drive off
bugs or season a sauce, and it really clears your sinus if you take a
way deep breath—"

Crushed leaves, the smell
reminds me of Annie—by the Big Sur river
she camped under laurel trees—all one summer
eating brown rice—naked—doing yoga—
her chanting, her way deep breath.

## Baking Bread

Warm sun of a farmyard    a huge old chestnut tree      just yesterday
the woman said      been raided by wild rhesus monkeys
we had boar meat, *inoshishi*, stewed with chestnuts      for lunch.
Deer, boar, monkeys, foxes    in these mountains
and lots of dams      little trucks on narrow winding roads

      Four hours from Tokyo
      brightly colored work clothes
      living on abandoned farms
      fighting concrete dams
    "I am hippy" says this woman
      baking bread

*(early October 2000 in the headwaters
of the Mibu River, Southern Japan Alps)*

# □ One Empty Bus

Jirka's place, a two-story farmhouse, the only one left in this narrow
mountain valley. Drive into the yard of cars and little trucks. Several
families sitting on the floor by the firepit, heavy board tables loaded
with local food. It's great to see Jirka again — he's Czech. He and his
Japanese wife have been here five years. Their daughter comes in,
lovely young woman glancing. Jirka says "she's shy" — she answers
firmly back in English, "Dad, I'm not shy!" Her name's "Akebi,"
flowering vine. I swap stories with the back country friends that
came to say hello, after years away. Upstairs was once a silk-worm
loft. Jirka and Etsuko weave rugs using goat hair from Greece. A
Rinzai priest from the nearby town drops in, planning a poetry
reading with our old friend Sansei. Bobbu sings Okinawan folk-
songs with that haunting falling close. Children sit closest to the
fire. Polished dark wood, sweet herb tea. Old house, new songs.
After eating and singing, it's dark. Need to keep moving — back
to the car —

On the night mountain canyon wall road
construction lights flash
we wait til the other lane comes through

one empty bus

*(early October 2000 in the headwaters
of the Mibu River, Southern Japanese Alps)*

# No Shadow

My friend Deane took me into the Yuba Goldfields. That's at the lower Yuba River outflow where it enters the Sacramento valley flatlands, a mile-wide stretch between grass and blue oak meadows. It goes on for ten miles. Here's where the mining tailings got dropped off by the wandering riverbed of the 1870s — forty miles downstream from where the giant hoses washed them off Sierra slopes.

We were walking on blue lupine-covered rounded hundred-foot gravel hills til we stood over the springtime rush of water. Watched a female osprey hunting along the main river channel. Her flight shot up, down, all sides, suddenly fell feet first into the river and emerged with a fish. Maybe fooling the fish by zigzagging, so — no hawk shadow. Carole said later, that's like trying to do zazen without your self entering into it.

> Standing on a gravel hill by the lower Yuba
> can see down west a giant airforce cargo plane from Beale
> hang-gliding down to land
> strangely slow over the tumbled dredged-out goldfields
> — practice run
> shadow of a cargo jet — soon gone
>
> no-shadow of an osprey
>
> still here

# □ Shandel

I gave a talk one outdoor evening to some students at a park. After, sitting on the bench and drinking juice, crowd chatting, a slender woman with dark hair came by and flashed a smile.

She had her daughter with her, maybe nine. Also dark short hair. Introduced her, "This is Shandel." I said "Please — tell me about the name Shandel." The mother sat on the bench beside me. "Shandel," she said, "is Yiddish — it means beautiful."

And then she pulled her daughter toward her, cupped her head in her hands and said "like a *shandel* head." And then she put her hands on the girl's cheeks and said "or a *shandel* face" — the young girl stood there smiling smiling sweetly at her mother.

"Why did you want to know?" the woman asked me. I told her "I once had a dear friend named Shandel who grew up in Greenwich Village. She was talented and lovely. I never heard the name again." —"It's not common — and Yiddish isn't either. I liked your talk — my daughter too."— they strolled away.

     People leaving in the dusk
     lights coming on, someone drumming in a cabin
     I remember Shandel saying
  "We were radicals and artists,
    I was the little princess of the Village —"
    at her home in San Francisco
    half a century ago.

# Night Herons

At Putah Creek a dense grove of live oaks. Step out of the sun and into the leafy low opening — from within the tree comes a steady banter, elusive little birds — they shift back, move up, stay out of sight. It's a great dark hall arched over with shimmering leaves — a high network of live oak limbs and twigs — four or five big trees woven together. Then see: a huge bird on a limb, head tucked under, motionless, sleeping. Peering deeper, seeing others — it's night herons! Roost by roost, settled in. One shifts a little, they know someone's here. Night herons passing the daylight hours in this hall of shadowy leaves.

Driving the 80 East, on the Bryte Bend bridge
high over the Sacramento River
wind-whipped by passing bigrigs,
　　　thinking of night herons
in a leafy palace, deep shade, by a pool.

*(Family Ardeidae, the black-crowned
night heron, Nycticorax nycticorax)*

# ◻ The Acropolis Back When

Toula Siete meets me on the street, she translates into Greek from
German and Italian. She and I are off to the Acropolis. We walk
through winding back streets and around the east end to the south
side walls and cliffs, go west past the semi-standing theater of
Dionysus. Reach up and pick some rotten shriveled olives — so bitter!

Up the steps to an outlook ledge, a glint of sunshine, and we are
above Athens. The modern city starts to fade. Toula's friend arrives
and leads us on steeper steps past the small shrine to Bear-girl
Artemis and into the territory of big clean slabs, pentelian marble,
old stone newly stacked — lintels perched on blocks, old talus tumble.

Walk the porch edge of the soaring Parthenon, sacred to gray-eyed
Athena. Slip into the restoration office by the cliff for tea. He is the
director of the restoration project for the whole show, especially the
Parthenon, Taso Tanoulas. He explicates the structures ruin by ruin,
and explains the calibrated aesthetics of just "leaving be." The city
racketing around below. Chilly breeze — now see the housecat tribe
gone wild in the scattered heaps of big stone blocks. This whole
hilltop a "palimpsest," Taso says, of buildings: Neolithic, Mycenean,
Periclean, and after. Then I'm thinking, here's a good place for a
bivouac — there's a spring, they say, a few yards down — people must
have camped here when —

> Lifetimes ago
> drawn to this rock
> I climbed it
> watched the clouds and the moon,
> slept the night.
>
> Dreamed of a gray-eyed girl
> on this rocky hill
> no buildings
> then

(1998)

# The Emu

Driving out of the foothills heading west—there's a high layer of cloud that's thin enough to let a lot of light through, not exactly sunshine but it showed up as 5 amps on the solar charge-controller at home. At about Truxell Road I slip seriously under the fog/cloud cover. Coming from up high like this, one knows that there are two layers of clouds, a high one and this low one. Closer to Davis, the belly of the cloud is almost on the ground and now it's fog.

In this drippy gloom I manage to pick up my laser printer, which has been repaired, buy a copy of *The Economist* at Newsbeat, get Korean-style ramen at the Asian store, and then cruise down to Red Rum Burger to try eating Ostrich.

Thinking back to the Emu: there it was last summer, an Emu in the yard with a green garter (probably an identification band, maybe with a serial number and a record of its shots). Our place surrounded by a dozen miles of forest. It soon ran off. I told Shawna about that—and she changed it into an Ostrich in her mind. As an Ostrich its picture got into a zine/comic poem, garter and all.

I'm recollecting all this as I eat my Ostrich burger at the place that now calls itself "Red Rum," which is "murder" backwards. Because for years it was called Murder Burger, until, I guess, there were just too many murders happening out there. The Ostrich burger is delicious. It's big, with lots of lettuce, onions, hot mustard, Swiss cheese, and sesame bun. In the midst of all those, you really don't taste Ostrich as anything special—it's just nice and chewy. I don't think they cook it rare. It is supposed to be good for you, low fat. And they don't use feedlots, so Ostriches probably eat lower on the food chain than steers that are being fattened on milo or corn for the slaughterhouse.

It certainly tastes just like Emu! Or vice versa. The Emu, a case of parallel evolution developing in far-off New Zealand. No garters there. But hold! Maoris might have tattooed some green designs right around those handsome thighs.


Lost Emu wandering the Sierra pine woods
      I have dressed you, tattooed you,
eaten you, spread wide your fame,
        in the time it takes to eat lunch

# ▫ The Hie Shrine and the "One-Tree" District

The Hie Jinja in Akasaka is on a rocky tree-covered *kopje* — skull-shaped little rocky hill and surrounded by an ocean of metropolis that stretches kilometers in all directions: urban buildings all sizes, broad traffic roads, narrow-lane neighborhoods, elevated speed-ways, criss-crossed underground subways. The great Diet buildings are to the north and beyond that the moated island of the Imperial Palace. The upscale Capital Tokyu Hotel just abutting the jinja is built on some land the shrine sold off. A giant ginkgo tree at the foot of the broad shrine stairs leads up into a forest of evergreen broad-leaved hardwoods and dense underbrush. At the top of the steps is a flat white gravel yard in front of the main shrine structure, wood all painted red.

Quarreling crows and crisp hopping sparrows, a dash of lizard. Green hill in the urban desert, "Island biogeography" — the shrews and geckos holed-up in the shrine-protected little forest, waiting for their time to come again. Down another set of steep steps and across the street below you go into the crowded "One-Tree" district with its many tiny multi-story buildings. Countless young Leisure Workers put out food and drink in thousands of bars til almost dawn.

> From the One-Tree bar district
> to the politics of parliament
> there's a shortcut over the hill
> up broad steep steps like
> crossing a pass
> and down the other side
>
> "Even though you may be busy
>     stop
> and make a little bow to the
> *San O*, the Mountain God
> of the Shrine"
> says a sign

## ◻ Cormorants

Dropping down rock ledges toward the breakers see a long flat point spiked with upright black cormorants and a few gulls gray and white. Rocks dabbed with threads and dribbles of bird-white. "White writing" like Mark Tobey did — drawn in loops and splatters — lime-rich droppings pointing back to the fishy waves.

Some rocks more decorated than others. A dark stink as the breeze rises, whiffs of ammonia — stabs you in the back brain — the only place worse once was on a fishing boat in the Gulf of Alaska — came alongside sea lion rocks and the whole thing blew in our face and whipped us with awful offal gassy blast.

Each bird-scholar has its own stone chair and the long full streaks below. Some rocks are unoccupied, unwritten.

Pelicans flap slow by. Cormorants fly clumsy — taking off from the water, drag their toes in the waves flap flap flap leaving scratch lines in the froth until they get just barely up and never fly much higher. Cormorants on a cliff launch out and fly downward til they drag their toes and then gain height again. Underwater they are fast as jets and full of grace.

> Toes writing in water
> rocks drawn with dribbles
> scat incense in the wind
> cormorants open their thin black wings
> talk about art, lecture the
> clouds of tiny fish

## ▫ To Go

Slopes of grassy mountains rise steep up from the narrow town
of Gorman north of LA on the route of the 5. Clusters of bush and
spans of spring wildflowers in bloom: California poppy, lupine,
paintbrush, fiddlebacks — blue, orange, and yellow — arching across
the slopes above. Afternoon angle to the sun. "Gorman" painted on
a hillside water tower. At Carl's Jr. in Gorman, getting coffee, I say
to the truck driver just parked on a slant and walked in behind me,
"those things are huge, how the hell do you drive them." He says,
"they're really easy." — "still, you have to find a place to park"—
He laughs, "yeah, you do."

       Heading north toward Tejon Pass
       humming ant-column vehicles
       six, eight lanes wide
       curving through a gap in the vertical
       cowflank-tan mountains, tops out of sight
       sprinkled with spring flowers

       bigrig parked by the water tower
       sun, cars, hills, coffee — all
       to go

# □ One Thousand Cranes

When Carole had a bad cancer prognosis some years back, several of her relatives got together and started folding the little *origami* called "cranes." They made one thousand paper cranes in different colors and sent them to us, it's a loving custom, to help one get well. Carole got better, though not cured, and they now hang in swooping strings like flowers on a wall in the house.

In East Asia cranes are noble birds of good fortune, suggesting long life, health, good luck, and troth. They are much in art. Most of the cranes of the world are now centered in Siberia and East Asia — they summer in the north, and winter in north India, eastern China, central Korea, and Japan's big south island, Kyushu.

There are two crane species in North America. One is the endangered whooping crane and the other the gray-beige sandhill crane. One group of sandhill cranes comes down to the Great Central Valley of California: an estimated 30,000 winter over in the area around Lodi, Cosumnes, Thornton, and west toward Walnut Grove. In late February I went with a friend to Cosumnes to look at the flocks of waterfowl one more time before they went back north. We found a place of flooded ricefields full of swimming white-fronted geese, ring-necked ducks, old squaws, teals, coots, and a few tundra swans. And then looking beyond them to a far levee there were rows of cranes pacing, eating, doing their leaping and bowing dance. "Staging up to go back north," they say.

A month later Carole and I were in Berkeley down on 4th Street where we saw an Asian crafts store called "One Thousand Cranes." It had that subtle incense and hinoki-wood aroma of old Japan. I asked the handsome Japanese woman "How do you say one thousand cranes?" She laughed and said *"senbazuru."* "Oh yes: one thousand *wings* of *tsuru*, cranes." And I told her that my wife and I lived in the Sierra Nevada and watch the cranes flying directly over our place. I remembered back to early March — Carole had been outside, I was in the shop. We began to hear the echoing crane calls. We saw a V — a V made of sub-Vs, flying northeast. They were way high but I did a count of a subsection and it came to eighty birds. They kept coming, echelon after echelon — the cranes just specks, but the echoing calls are loud. More grand flying wedges all afternoon — at least a thousand cranes.

So I told the lady of the store, "Not long ago we watched the cranes go over heading north. They came by all afternoon, at least a thousand." The woman smiled. "Of course. Real life cranes. Good luck for all of us, good luck for you."

<br>

From the shady toolshed
hear those "gr r u  gr u u  g rr ruu"
calls from the sky
step out and squint at the bright
      nothing in sight
just odd far calls
echoing, faint,
*grus canadensis*
heading north
       one mile high

# □ For Anthea Corinne Snyder Lowry

*1932–2002*

She was on the Marin County Grand Jury, heading to a meeting,
south of Petaluma on the 101. The pickup ahead of her lost a grass-
mower off the back. She pulled onto the shoulder, and walked right
out into the lane to take it off. That had always been her way. Struck
by a speedy car, an instant death.

> White egrets standing there
> always standing there
> there at the crossing
>
> on the Petaluma River

# ◦ The Great Bell of the Gion

*"The great bell of the Gion Temple reverberates into every human heart to wake us to the fact that all is impermanent and fleeting. The withered flowers of the sâla trees by Shakyamuni's deathbed remind us that even those flourishing with wealth and power will soon pass away. The life of fame and pride is as ephemeral as a springtime dream. The courageous and aggressive person too will vanish like a swirl of dust in the wind."*        —*The Heike Monogatari, 12th century*

Heading back to our little house in Murasakino from the Gion Shrine on New Year's eve, with a glowing wick handout from a priest—lit in the New Year sacred fire started anew by bow drill, purified. Walking and lightly swinging the long wick to keep it aglow, in a crowd of people whirling wicks and heading home, finally catch a taxi. Once home start a propane gasplate from the almost-gone wick. Now, a sacred fire in the house. The Gion's huge bell still ringing in the new year: as soft, as loud, at the house three kilometers away as it was at the temple.

> Up along the Kamo River
> northwest to higher ground.
> After midnight New Year's eve:
> the great bell of the Gion
> one hundred eight times
> deeply booms through town.
> From across the valley
> it's a dark whisper
> echoing in your liver,
> mending your
>         fragile heart.

*(Gion Park, Shrine, & Temple in Eastern Kyoto, named for the park, monastery, and bell of Jetavana in India, south of Shravasti, where the Buddha sometimes taught)*

# VI

## After Bamiyan

# □ After Bamiyan

March 2001

The Chinese Buddhist pilgrim Hsüan Tsang described the giant, gleaming, painted carved-out Buddhas standing in their stone cave-niches at the edge of the Bamiyan Valley as he passed through there on foot, on his way to India in the seventh century CE. Last week they were blown up by the Taliban. Not just by the Taliban, but by woman-and-nature-denying authoritarian worldviews that go back much farther than Abraham. Dennis Dutton sent this poem around:

> Not even
> under mortar fire
> do they flinch.
> The Buddhas of Bamiyan
> Take Refuge in the dust.

May we keep our minds clear and calm and in the present moment, and honor the dust.

□ □ □

April 2001

From a man who writes about Buddhism

> Dear Gary:
> Well, yes, but, the manifest Dharma is intra-samsaric, and will decay.
> —R.
> —I wrote back,
> Ah yes . . . impermanence. But this is never a
reason to let compassion and focus slide, or to pass off the sufferings of others because they are merely impermanent beings. Issa's haiku goes,

> *Tsuyu no yo wa        tsuyu no yo nagara        sarinagara*

> "This dewdrop world
> is but a dewdrop world
> and yet—"

That *"and yet"* is our perennial practice. And maybe the root of the Dharma.

□ □ □

A person who should know better wrote, "Many credulous and sentimental Westerners, I suspect, were upset by the destruction of the Afghan Buddha figures because they believe that so-called Eastern religion is more tender-hearted and less dogmatic . . . So— is nothing sacred? Only respect for human life and culture, which requires no divine sanction and no priesthood to inculcate it. The foolish veneration of holy places and holy texts remains a principal obstacle to that simple realization."

—"This is another case of 'blame the victim'" I answered. "Buddhism is not on trial here. The Bamiyan statues are part of human life and culture, they are works of art, being destroyed by idolators of the book. Is there anything 'credulous' in respecting the art and religious culture of the past? Counting on the tender-heartedness of (most) Buddhists, you can feel safe in trashing the Bamiyan figures as though the Taliban wasn't doing a good enough job. I doubt you would have the nerve to call for launching a little missile at the Ka'aba. There are people who would put a hit on you and you know it."

□ □ □

September 2001

> The men and women who
> died at the World Trade Center
> together with the
> Buddhas of Bamiyan,
> Take Refuge in the dust.

## □ Loose on Earth

A tiny spark, or
the slow-moving glow on the fuse
creeping toward where
ergs held close

in petrol, saltpeter, mine gas,
buzzing minerals in the ground,
are waiting.

Held tight in a few hard words
in a dark mood,
in an old shame.

Humanity,
      said Jeffers, is like a quick

explosion on the planet
we're loose on earth
half a million years
our weird blast spreading —

and after,
rubble — millennia to weather,
soften, fragment,
sprout, and green again

## ▫ Falling from a Height, Holding Hands

What was *that*?
storms of flying glass
& billowing flames

a clear day to the far sky—

better than burning,
hold hands.

We will be
two     peregrines     diving

all the way down

# The Kannon of Asakusa,
## Sensō-ji    Short Grass Temple
## Sumida River

At the Buddha-hall of Sensō-ji
hundreds of worshippers surge up the high stone steps,
into the hall dropping coins in the bin—
look into the black-and-gold chambers, somewhere a statue
of Kannon, Kuan-yin, Goddess of Mercy,
Avalokiteshvara Bodhisattva,
peace and compassion for all in this world-realm
          this particular time,
old and young people swirl by. Incense in clouds.
We follow the flow out the south side steps,
white gravels, and back down the pilgrim
stone walkway that leads there
lined with street shops and stalls, packed with
babies in strollers, old folks in wheelchairs, girls in their tanktops
back to the gate at the entrance.

Gold Dragon Mountain, Thunder Gate,
red tree pillars and sweeping tile eaves—
back out to the streets: traffic, police, taxis,
tempura restaurants of Edo.
Cross to the riverside park space,
men cross-legged on cardboard under the shade tree
and step into the long slender riverboat water-bus
that runs down the Sumida River.

I came here unwitting, the right way,
ascending the Sumidagawa, approaching Sensō-ji from the sea.
Under the Thunder Gate, walking the pilgrim path,
climbing the steps to

Avalokiteshvara, Bodhisattva of Compassion,
asking: please guide us through samsara.

        ("Form, sensation, thought, impulse, consciousness,
                    are not born, not destroyed,
                            without gain, without loss
no hindrance! Thus no fear.")

For all beings
living or not,     beings or not,

inside  or   outside of time

### A Turning Verse for the Billions of Beings

We have spoken again the unknown words of the spell
that purifies the world
turning its virtue and power back     over
to those who died in wars — in the fields — on the seas
and to the billions of spirits in the realms of
form, of no-form, or in the realm of hot desire.

Hail all true and grounded beings
in all directions,     in the realms of form,
of no-form, or of hot desire

hail all noble woke-up big-heart beings;
*hail* — great wisdom of the path that goes beyond

*Mahāprajñāpāramitā*

*(from the Chinese)*

*Mount St. Helens, August 1945, by G.S.*

# Notes

*"Letting Go"*
The person who was calmly calling radio information in on his two-way radio was Gerald Martin at a site two miles north of Coldwater II station and seven miles from the crater. He was a retired navy radioman volunteer from Southern California. The very first victim of the blast was volcanologist David Johnston, who was on watch at the Coldwater II Observation Post. He radioed the famous message "Vancouver! Vancouver! This is it!" at 8:32 AM on May 18, 1980. His station was vaporized. The viewpoint is now known as Johnston Ridge.

*"Pearly Everlasting"*
". . . that big party Siddhartha went to on the night he left the house for good" is a reference to a passage in Ashvaghosha's *Acts of the Buddha* (Skt *Buddhacharita*), second century CE, describing the conclusion of an evening's entertainment in the palace. Siddhartha's many beautiful companions had finally all fallen asleep on the floor in various relaxed postures. Siddhartha, still awake, paced among them thinking, "Even the liveliest pleasures of privileged young people come to this!" or somesuch, and went down to the stable, got a horse, and rode into the forest. Cutting off his hairdo, practicing yoga and austerities, and learning to meditate, he eventually accomplished realization and became the "Enlightened One"—"The Buddha."

*"One Thousand Cranes"*
With regard to the sandhill crane color "gray-beige," the closest color in the Methuen *Handbook of Color* would be saruk (6E3), from *Saruq*, an Iranian village where it is a traditional color for rugs. The French derivation is *saroque*, or *saroq*.

*"The Great Bell of the Gion"*
The large Gion Park, shrine, and temple complex is one of the loveliest features of the eastern edge of Kyoto, the old capital of Japan. It stretches along the lower slopes of the hills. It is named for the grounds and monastery of Jetavana that were on the outskirts of the ancient Indian city of Shravasti. Jetavana was a favorite stopping place of the historical Buddha: he spent nineteen rainy seasons there. Jetavana was a site of many teachings, and is said to have had a great bell.

*"Sensō-ji"*

This popular Buddhist temple is commonly referred to as the "Asakusa Kannon-dera," that is, the "Kannon temple of the Asakusa district." Asakusa means "short grass" as does the "sensō" in "Sensō-ji." The whole neighborhood, on the right bank of the Sumida River, has long been famous for its countless little shops, temples, parks, and popular amusements.

In the seventh century three fishermen pulled in their net and found a Kannon image in it. They first enshrined it in a little hut. This was the beginning of what was to become a great temple, the earliest in Edo (old Tokyo). Soon there were many other Buddhist images on the altar besides the first little one (supposedly only 2.1 inches tall)—a Kannon, a Fudo, an Aizen, and much more. All of it went up in flames during World War II. The rebuilt temple has the old-style power and beauty. Throngs of pilgrims and visitors are constantly coming and going.

# Thanks To

Especially:
— Carole Koda, ever so
Jack Shoemaker — comrade and publisher
Fred Swanson — scientist, philosopher, walker

Aki Tamura and the people of Oshika village
Bob Uchida, poet-musician
Deane Swickard
Dennis Dutton for his Bamiyan poem
Eldridge Moores
Gary Holthaus
Henry Zenk, for his help with Sahaptin place names and the name "Loowit"
Isabel Stirling for research help and advice
Jean Koda
Jirka Wein, of Praha and the Southern Japan Alps
Kai Snyder
Katsu Yamazato of Naha
Ko Un of Seoul
Lee Gurga
Liana Sakeliou of Athens
Misa Honde of Kobe
Morio Takizawa of Tokyo
Nanao Sakaki, for his translation of Issa's "snail," nine bows
Peter Matthiessen
Satoru Mishima of the Kanto Plain
Shawna Ryan for ostrich and emu
Shige Hara
Steve Antler and Carla Jupiter, and the house above the river
Steve Eubanks for the Star Fire
Ursula LeGuin for her fine rare book on Mt. St. Helens, *In the Red Zone*
Young poets of Putah-toi, sitting on the summer dust

# Acknowledgments

Some of the poems in *Danger on Peaks* have appeared in the following publications. We thank the editors and publishers of these periodicals and books for their good work.

"Acropolis Back When"— selection as "Acropolis Hill" in *Metre* no. 7/8 Spring Summer 2000 (England); and *Facture* 2, 2001.

"After Bamiyan"— *Reed*, February 2002.

"Ankle-deep in Ashes"— *Tree Rings* no. 16, January 2004.

"Baking Bread"— Poison Oak broadside, Tangram Press, May 2003.

"Carwash Time," "Flowers in the Night Sky," "Brighter Yellow," and "To the Liking of Salmon"— *Tule Review* IV.1, Issue 30, Winter 2003.

"Claws/Cause"— *Shambhala Sun*, October 2002.

"Coffee, Markets, Blossoms"— *Facture* 2, 2001.

"For Philip Zenshin Whalen"— as a broadside by Tangram Press, 2002.

"How Many?"— *Facture* 2, 2001.

"Icy Mountains Constantly Walking"— *The Gary Snyder Reader* (Counterpoint, 1999).

"In the Santa Clarita Valley"— *Facture* 2, 2001.

"Night Herons"— *Where Do I Walk?*— ed. Maria Melendez, Brooke Byrd, and Adam Smith. UC Davis Arboretum, 2003.

"One Thousand Cranes"— *The Phoebe*, Sierra Foothills Audubon Society, X.03 Vol. 24.6, Nov-Dec 2003.

"Out of the underbrush," "Chainsaw dust," "Hammering a dent out of a bucket," and "Baby jackrabbit on the ground"— *Modern Haiku* XXXII.3 Fall 2001.

"Sensō-ji" and "The Great Bell of the Gion"— *Kyoto Review*, 2005.

"Snow Flies, Burn Brush, Shut Down"— *Van Gogh's Ear* (Paris) Spring 2002; broadside by Ken Sanders, Dream Garden Books, February 2003.

"Summer of '97"— *The Gary Snyder Reader* (Counterpoint, 1999).

"To Go"— *Orion*, July-August 2004.

"Waiting for a Ride"— *The New Yorker*, August 2004.

"What to Tell, Still"— *Sulfur* 45/46 Spring 2000; and *Look Out* (New Directions, 2002).

"Winter Almond" and "To All the Girls Whose Ears I Pierced Back Then"— *Salt Lick Quarterly* (Australia).